A Photographic Tribute to

Biblical Women

By April Craig

CMH Legacy Publications

It is my hope that as individuals look through this book, they will gain a love of the scriptures and have a deeper desire to draw closer to Jesus Christ. ~April Craig

www.aprilcraig.com

ISBN: 978-0-9858210-0-5
Library of Congress Control Number: 2012911624

CMH Legacy Publications
Newnan, Georgia

First Printing: July 2012
Printed in the United States of America
by RJ Communications, NY, NY
For more information call: 1-800-621-2556
Batch: 0712

This book was printed in compliance with the CPSIA laws and regulations.

Acknowledgements

I would like to thank my mother-in-law, Connie Craig, for the countless hours of sewing, encouragement, and motivation she put into this project. The hours we spent together filled the void that was left after losing my mother last year. Thank you for taking on the role of mom and grandma two-fold in her absence. I am truly blessed to have your influence in my life. I know my mom smiled down on us from heaven as we worked together to finish this book. I'd also like to thank my father-in-law, Tommy Craig, for sharing his talent with wood and metal to help create props.

A special thank you to Dan Glass, who for years has patiently taught me everything I know about photography. My gratitude is indescribable for the hours you have invested in tutoring me and editing images. Without your help, this book would not have been possible!

I give credit to Carrie Mapp for giving me the idea for this book and for the hours she and her husband, Mark, spent helping with photo sessions. Thank you to Carrie Mapp and Jenny Cowdell for helping me wrangle children and pose newborns. I will miss our girls' days out shopping for just the right fabric for costumes and then grabbing lunch before our little ones got home from school.

I'd like to express appreciation to my father for watching my little ones during the photo sessions and countless hours I spent at the computer editing. I'm pretty sure I owe you a dozen boxes of corn dogs and cookies by now. You are the best "Saypa" ever!

I express my gratitude to my husband, whom I've started calling, "My Iron Man" (quite literally). He spent many hours ironing the costumes the night before each session. Thank you sweetheart for being a constant support and for taking on more of the workload at home while I labored on this project. You are my best friend. Life is a beautiful journey with you by my side!

Thank you to Julie Thompson for editing the text. What a powerful example of charity you are in my life! Thank you for sharing your talent and knowledge. Thank you to Robin for your enthusiasm in helping with the costume fabrics. Thank you to Ginger for your extraordinary jewelry suggestions. Thank you to Amber and Martin Hodges, for making this book a possibility!

Most importantly, I humbly express gratitude to the Lord for my talent and for providing those who have helped me to develop it. It's my hope that in publishing this book, many individuals will come to know the love the Lord has for each of us. That as we search the scriptures with our children, they will know without a doubt where they should look for their salvation, even to Jesus Christ.

Models

I'd like to thank each of my models and their families. It amazed me time and again how these children would get into their costumes and fall completely into character. Their innocence and purity brought a sweet spirit of reverence into my studio. I was continually humbled and uplifted during my hours of editing as I would gaze into their faces and truly see the light of Christ shining in their countenances. I'm so thankful for the Spirit that attended us during this project. It reminds me of a favorite verse:

"Jesus said, Suffer little children, and forbid them not, to come unto me: for of such is the kingdom of heaven."
~Matthew 19:14

Kiaran Beckwith	Emily Cotrell	Luke Hanks	Ian McLay
Sierra Bowron	Kaley Cotrell	Victoria Hanks	Kaleb McLay
Brooklyn Brandley	Courtney Cowdell	Cael Jessup	Chandley Ohman
Cierra Byrd	Logan Cowdell	Jace Jessup	Billie Otte
Abby Caldwell	Samantha Cowdell	Jaxon Jessup	Tobie Otte
Amanda Caldwell	Anna Craig	Zaden Jessup	Miriam Padgett
Jordan Clark	Autumn Craig	Annabel Jewkes	Caique Paraense
Payton Clark	Lillian Craig	Ryan Johnson	Emma Patterson
Ethan Clarke	Martin David Craig, Jr.	Colin Langley	Laura Grace Sears
Kaylin Clarke	Slater Craig	Madilyn Langley	Katelyn Singleton
Mika Clarke	Davi DeWeese	Haley Mapp	Rafe Sipes
Weston Clarke	Fadrah Edwards	Meredith Matheny	Emma Spokes
Daniel Coates	Iliana Garcia	Amelia McLay	Noah Thomas
Ashley Cotrell	Caroline Hanks	Hannah McLay	Ruby Thompson

Models ranged in age from 8 days to 18 years with the exception of my sweet model, Mrs. Allison Anderson, which depicted Sarah holding baby Isaac. Models are listed alphabetically.

This book is dedicated to my children:
Tiffany, Kent, Zachary, Lillian, Slater, and Autumn.
May the scriptures give you direction,
bring you comfort, and draw you closer to your Savior.

Scripture references are from the
King James Version of the Bible.

A Photographic Tribute to

Biblical Women

*"Train up a child in
the way he should go:
and when he is old, he
will not depart from it."*

Proverbs 22:6

Eve's

story helps us
understand that even
though our lives
are full of difficult
choices our
Father in Heaven
has given us a way
to return to Him
through the saving
grace of Jesus Christ.

Genesis
3:6

"Behold the
Lamb of God,
which taketh away
the sin of the world."
John 1:29

Sarah's

story teaches us to
believe in
God's miracles.
Through our
faith and
with patience,
we discover all
things are possible
with the Lord.

Genesis:
17: 15-17

"Is any thing too hard
for the Lord?"
Genesis 18:14

Rebekah's journey

began with a simple act of kindness.
She set a wonderful example of service.

Genesis 24: 15-20

Rachel, Beloved Wife of Jacob

Genesis 29: 11-20

"And Jacob served seven years for Rachel; and they seemed unto him but a few days, for the love he had to her."

Rachel was barren for years before she had her first son, Joseph. Jacob loved Joseph more than all his other children and made him a coat of many colors.

Leah, Mother of Nations

She gave birth to royal and priestly bloodlines:
Reuben, Simeon, Levi, Judah, Issachar, Zebulun, and Dinah.

Genesis 30: 19-21

Shiphrah and Puah

Hebrew Midwives
Exodus 1:15-22

These midwives were ordered by the King to kill all the baby boys born to Hebrew women. But the midwives feared God, and did not listen to the King.

"Choose you this day whom ye will serve...but as for me and my house we will serve the Lord."
Joshua 24: 15

Miriam with Moses

My Brother's Keeper

Miriam watched over her little brother by the river's brink
until he was discovered by Pharaoh's daughter and
arranged for her mother to be his nursemaid.

Exodus 2:1-10

Daughters of Zelophehad

These sisters stood together and petitioned for their rights as women to receive an inheritance. The Lord told Moses that the daughters were right, and then the law was changed for them to receive a portion of their father's possessions.

Numbers 27: 1-11

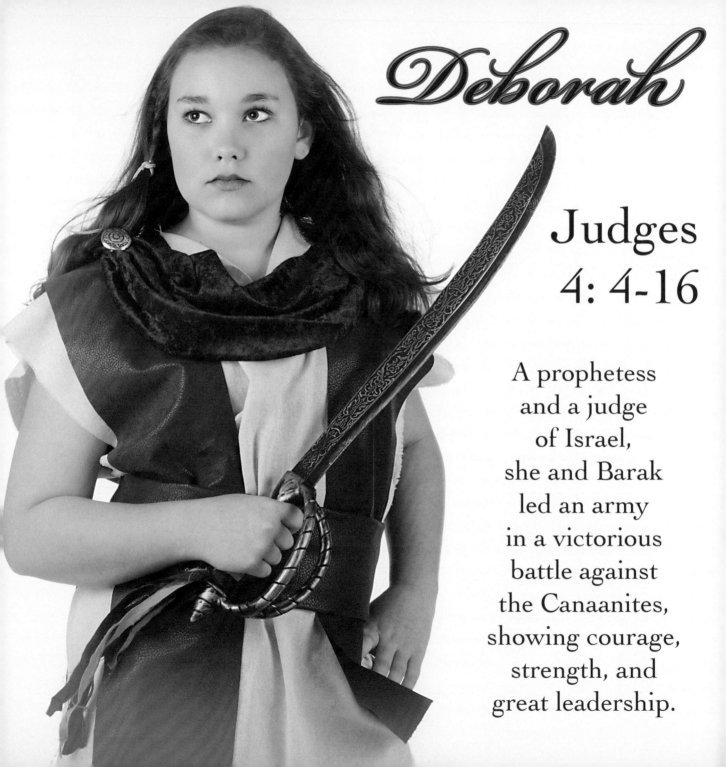

Deborah

Judges 4: 4-16

A prophetess
and a judge
of Israel,
she and Barak
led an army
in a victorious
battle against
the Canaanites,
showing courage,
strength, and
great leadership.

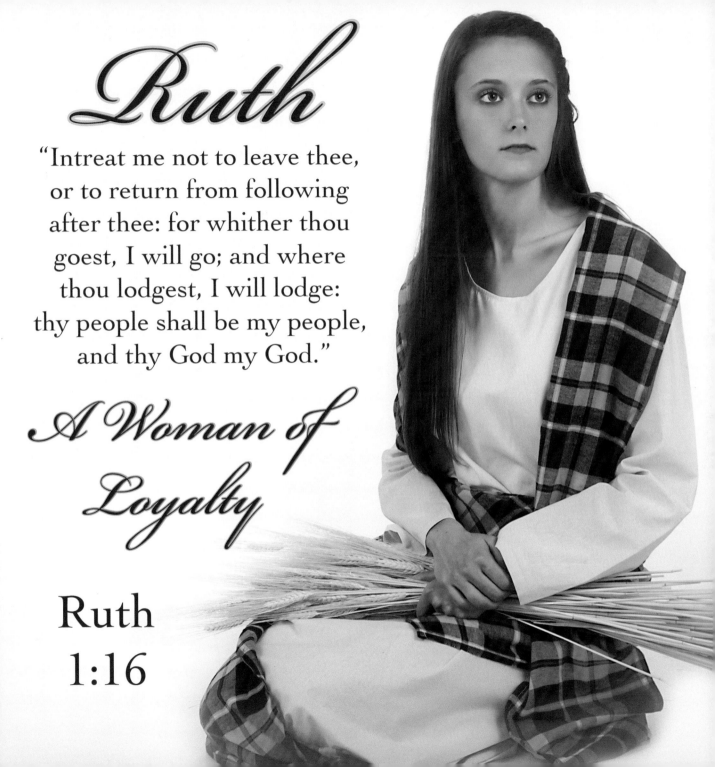

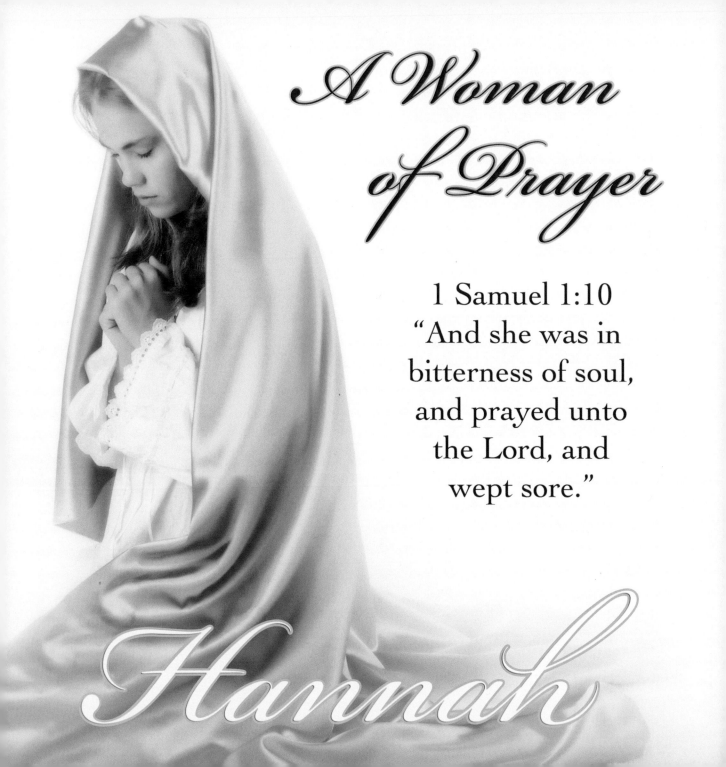

A Woman of Prayer

1 Samuel 1:10
"And she was in bitterness of soul, and prayed unto the Lord, and wept sore."

Hannah

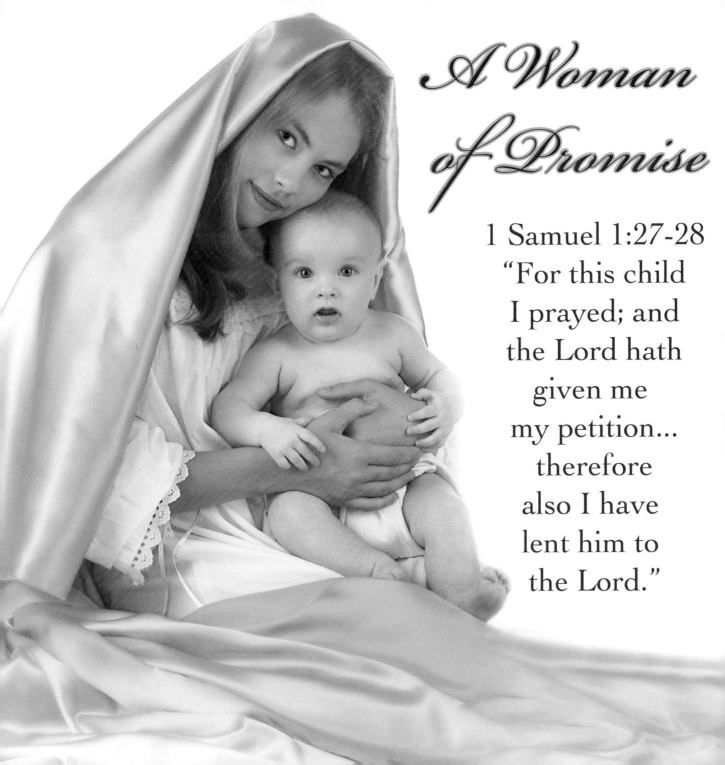

A Woman
of Promise

1 Samuel 1:27-28
"For this child
I prayed; and
the Lord hath
given me
my petition...
therefore
also I have
lent him to
the Lord."

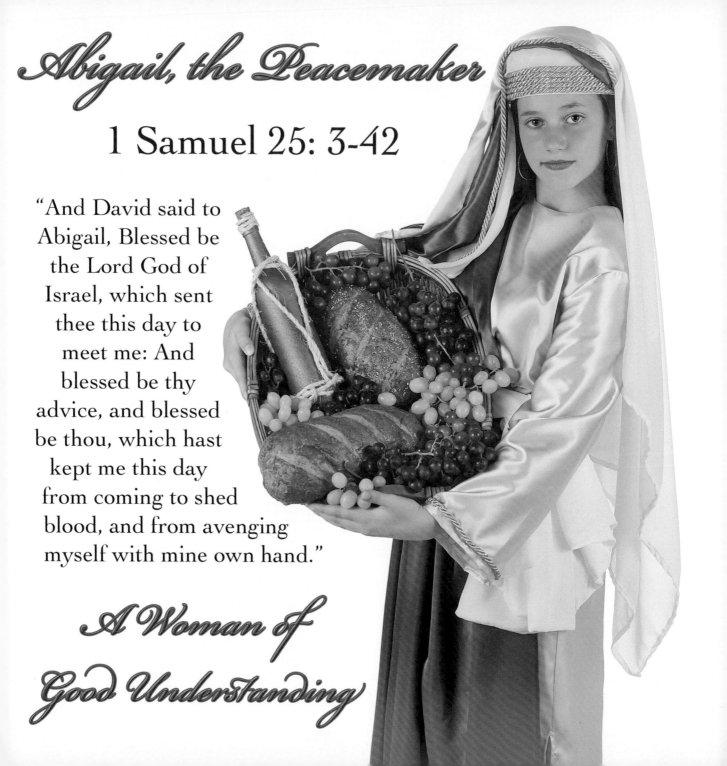

Abigail, the Peacemaker

1 Samuel 25: 3-42

"And David said to Abigail, Blessed be the Lord God of Israel, which sent thee this day to meet me: And blessed be thy advice, and blessed be thou, which hast kept me this day from coming to shed blood, and from avenging myself with mine own hand."

A Woman of Good Understanding

Widow of Zarephath

This woman had great faith and a heart willing to sacrifice. She gave the last of her food to sustain the prophet Elijah when she and her son were about to starve.

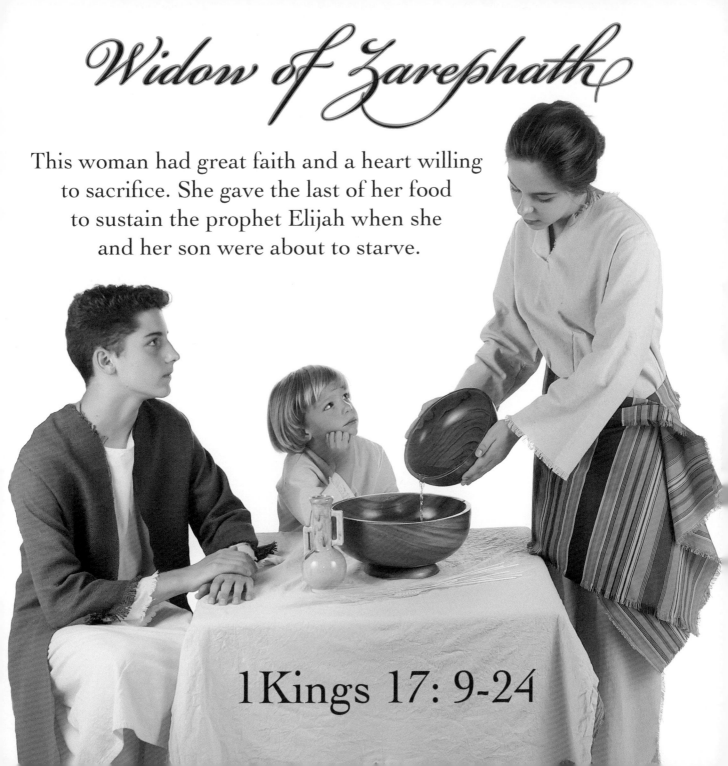

1 Kings 17: 9-24

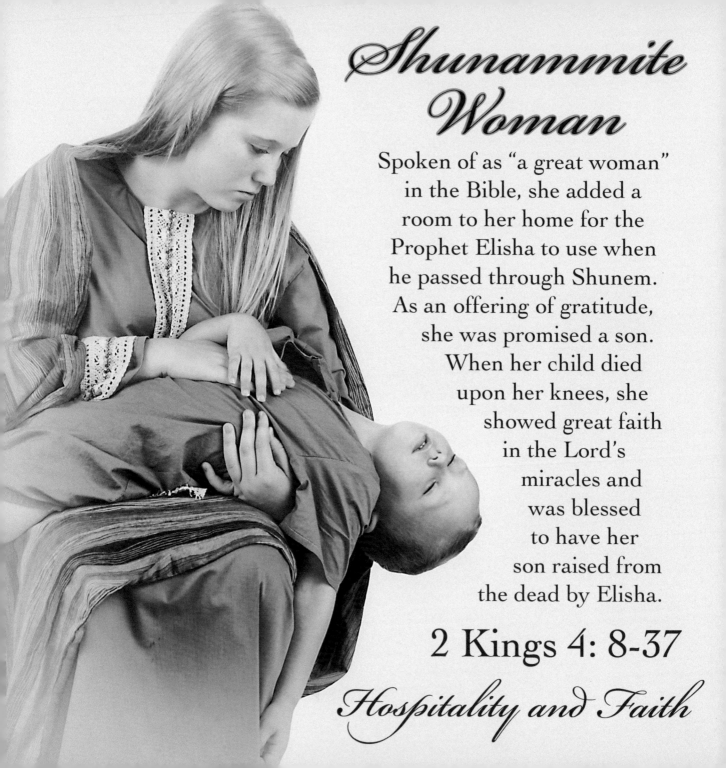

Shunammite Woman

Spoken of as "a great woman" in the Bible, she added a room to her home for the Prophet Elisha to use when he passed through Shunem. As an offering of gratitude, she was promised a son. When her child died upon her knees, she showed great faith in the Lord's miracles and was blessed to have her son raised from the dead by Elisha.

2 Kings 4: 8-37

Hospitality and Faith

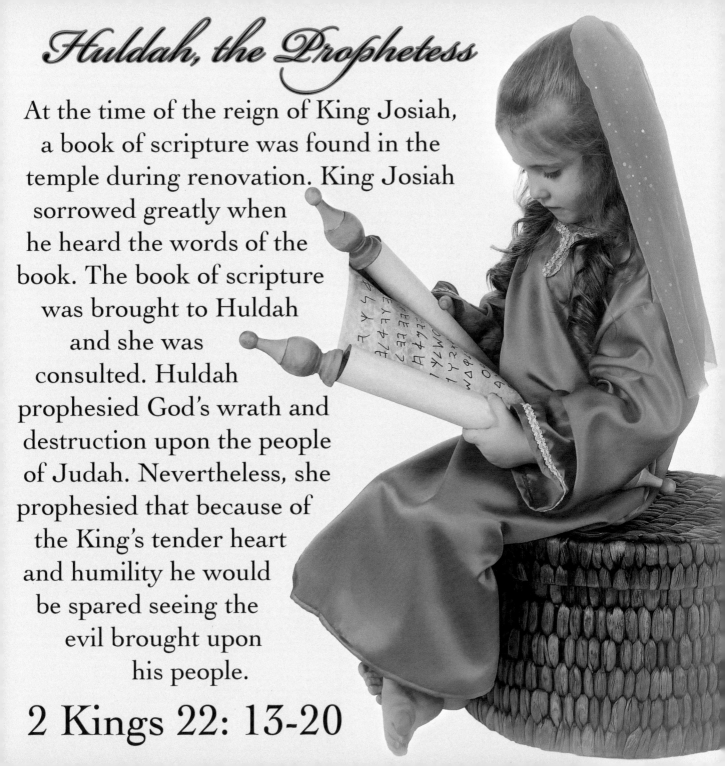

Huldah, the Prophetess

At the time of the reign of King Josiah, a book of scripture was found in the temple during renovation. King Josiah sorrowed greatly when he heard the words of the book. The book of scripture was brought to Huldah and she was consulted. Huldah prophesied God's wrath and destruction upon the people of Judah. Nevertheless, she prophesied that because of the King's tender heart and humility he would be spared seeing the evil brought upon his people.

2 Kings 22: 13-20

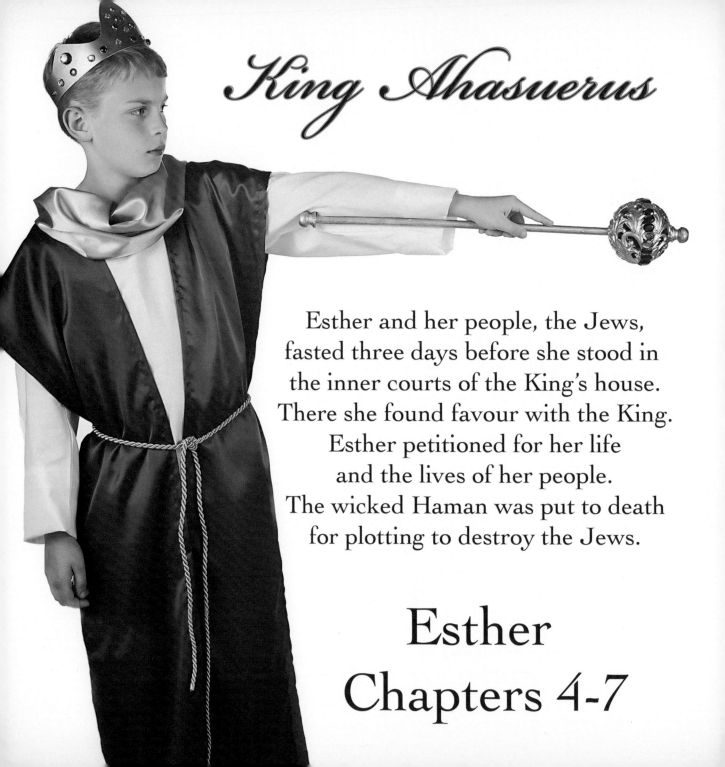

King Ahasuerus

Esther and her people, the Jews,
fasted three days before she stood in
the inner courts of the King's house.
There she found favour with the King.
Esther petitioned for her life
and the lives of her people.
The wicked Haman was put to death
for plotting to destroy the Jews.

Esther
Chapters 4-7

Esther

risked her life
to save her people.

Esther
5:1-3

Woman of
Courage

Mary, the Mother of Jesus

Luke 1:28

"And the angel came in unto her, and said, Hail, thou that art highly favoured, the Lord is with thee: blessed art thou among women."

Noble Motherhood

Mary and Martha

Luke 10: 38-42

With many good and worthy
things to draw our
time and attention, these
biblical sisters remind
us about priorities.
We learn that one
thing is needful:
to seek after that
better part, which is
Jesus Christ.

"Seek ye first

the kingdom of
God, and his
righteousness;
and all these
things shall be
added unto you."

Matthew 6:33

Widow's Mite

"And there came a certain
poor widow, and she
threw in two mites,
which make
a farthing."
And Jesus said,
"Verily I say
unto you, That this
poor widow hath
cast more in, than all
they which have cast into
the treasury: For all they
did cast in of their
abundance; but she of
her want did cast in
all that she had,
even all her living."

Mark 12: 41-44

Parable of the 10 Virgins

"And five of them were wise, and five were foolish.
They that were foolish took their lamps, and took no oil with them:
But the wise took oil in their vessels with their lamps."

Women of Preparedness

Matthew 25: 1-13

"Watch therefore, for ye know neither the day nor the hour wherein the Son of man cometh."

Woman of Faith

"And a certain woman, which had
an issue of blood twelve years...
For she said, If I may touch
but his clothes, I shall be whole."

And Jesus said unto her,
"Daughter, thy faith
hath made thee whole;
go in peace, and be
whole of thy plague."

Mark
5: 25-34

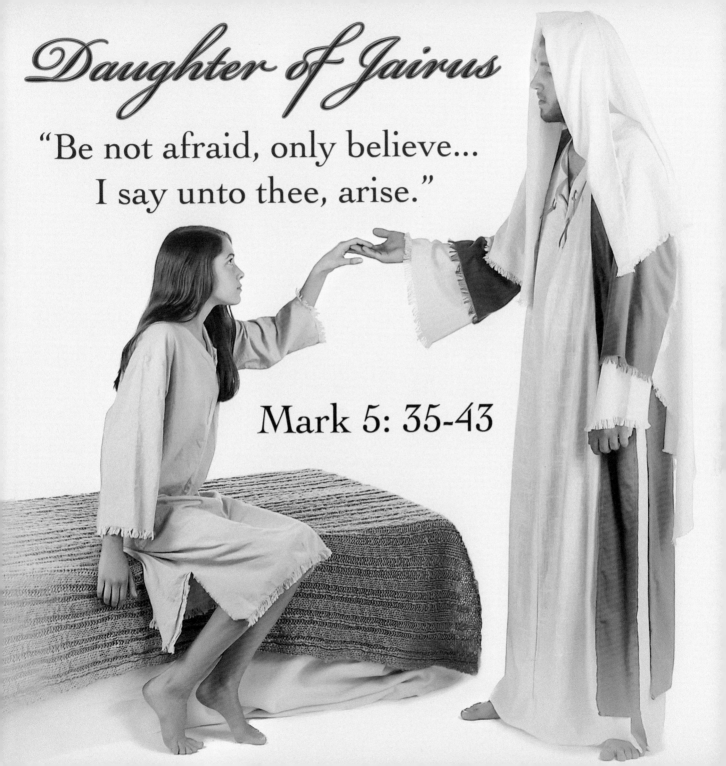

Samaritan Woman at the Well

Jesus said, "Whosoever drinketh of this water shall thirst again: But whosoever drinketh of the water that I shall give him shall never thirst; but the water that I shall give him shall be in him a well of water springing up into everlasting life."

John 4: 5-42

Partaker of Living Water

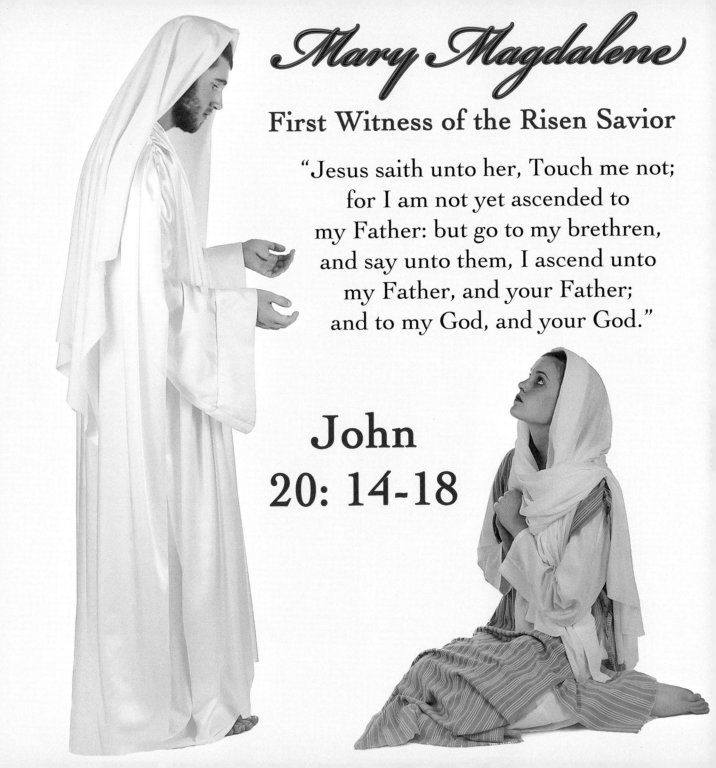

Mary Magdalene

First Witness of the Risen Savior

"Jesus saith unto her, Touch me not;
for I am not yet ascended to
my Father: but go to my brethren,
and say unto them, I ascend unto
my Father, and your Father;
and to my God, and your God."

John
20: 14-18

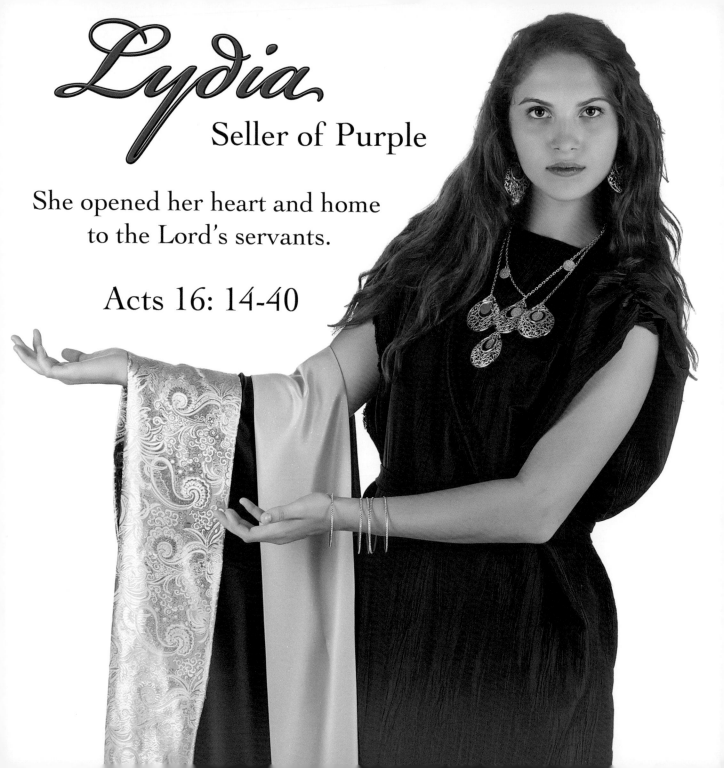

Daughter of God

Romans 8:16 "The Spirit itself beareth witness with
our spirit, that we are the children of God."

Every little girl represents a biblical woman as a child of God.
Heavenly Father loves us and wants all of His children
to return to live with Him again.

Armor of *God*

Helmet
of Salvation

Breastplate
of Righteousness

Shield
of Faith

Loins
Girt with Truth

Ephesians
6: 11-17

Sword
of the Spirit

Feet
Gospel of
Peace

Praying Always

Men and women
have a responsibility
to put on the
whole armor of God
that we may be able
to stand against
the evil influences
of Satan to
protect our families!

Ephesians
6:18